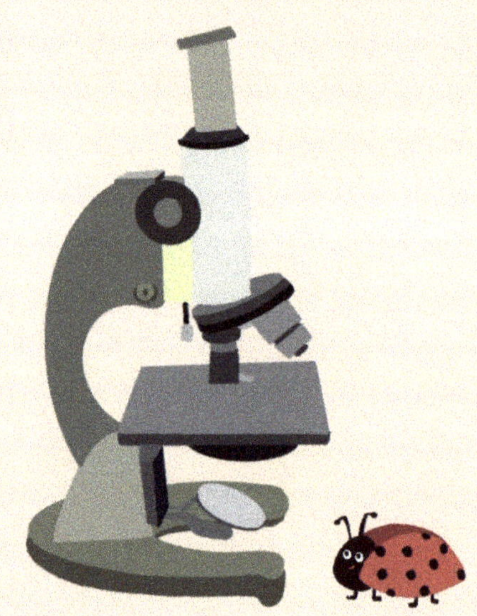

Bugs in My Tummy

Alana C. Marks
Illustrator: Noor Zaki

Alana C. Marks, LLC-Ohio

Alana C. Marks, LLC
Waterville, Ohio, USA

Library of Congress Control Number: 2024919636
Names: Marks, Alana C., 2024-author
Title: Bugs in My Tummy/Alana C. Marks.
Audience: Aged 3-5
Summary: "Too many bad germs in your tummy will make you sick. It's important that you wash your hands."
Identifiers: LCCN 2024919636
ISBN print: 979-8-9912730-2-2
ISBN Kindle: 979-8-9912730-3-9
ISBN (epub) 979-8-9912730-4-6
BISAC: JNF024060   JUVENILE NONFICTION / Health & Daily Living / Personal Hygiene

Manufactured in the United States of America

Did you know you have bugs in your tummy?

3

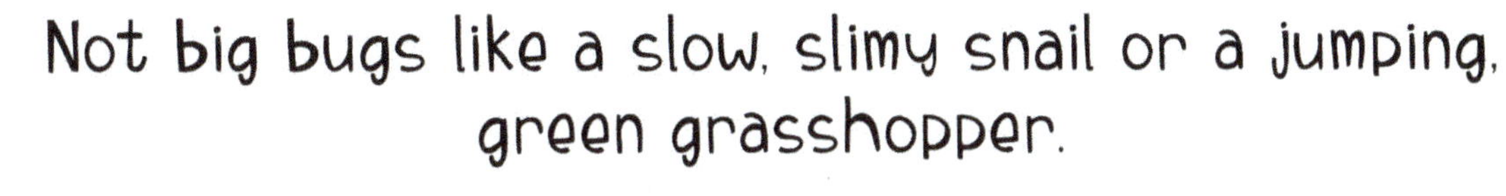

Not big bugs like a slow, slimy snail or a jumping, green grasshopper.

Not little bugs like a brown, slithering earthworm or a
black-spotted red ladybug.

6

Not even tiny bugs like a busy army ant or a bitsy, black spider.

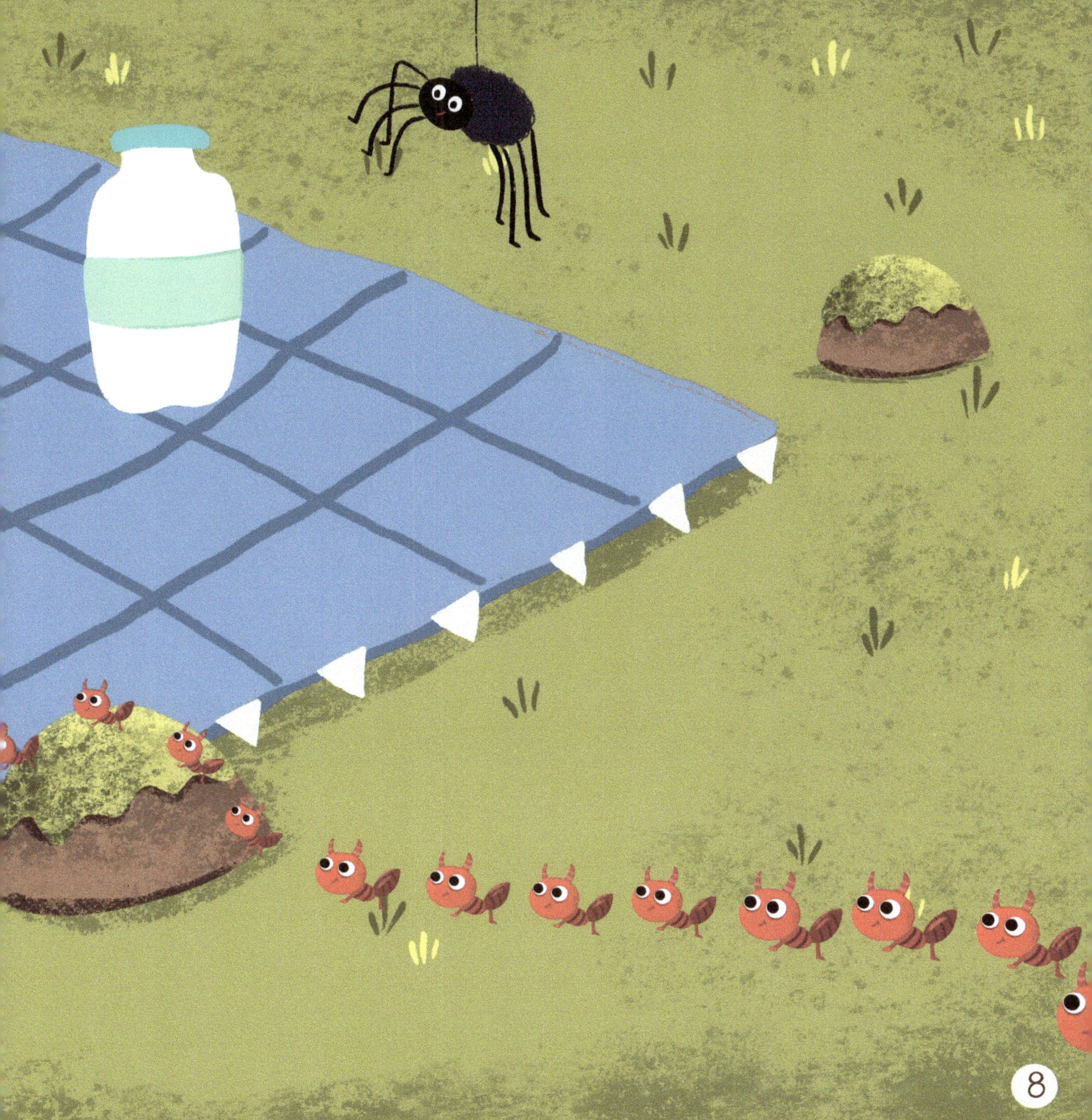

The bugs in your tummy are so teeny-weeny you cannot see them with only your eyes.

2

You need a microscope. A microscope helps you see teeny-weeny things.

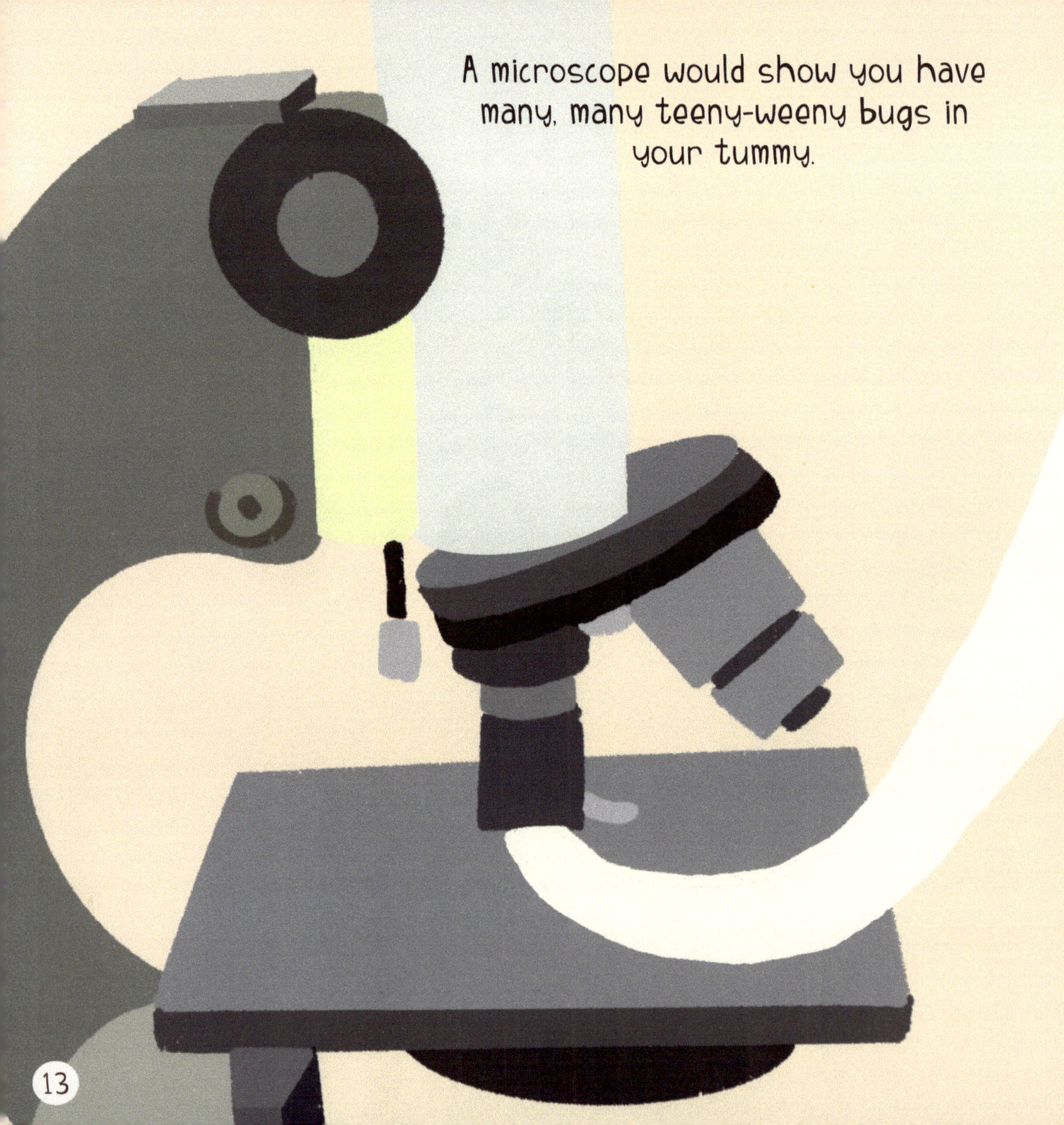
A microscope would show you have
many, many teeny-weeny bugs in
your tummy.

13

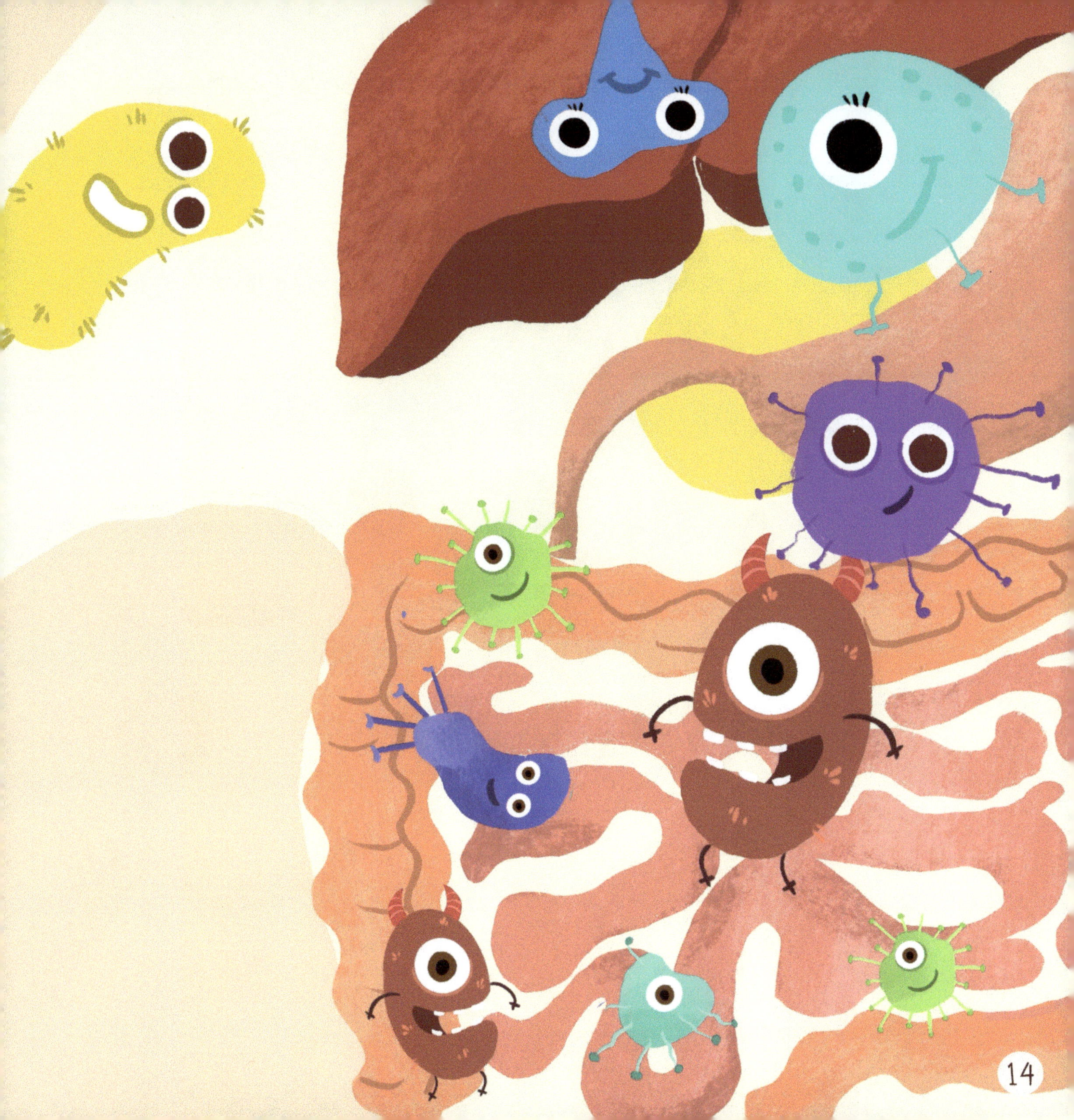

The bugs in your tummy are called germs. Good germs help keep your body healthy.

Some make special vitamins to help you stop bleeding when you cut your finger or skin your knee.

18

Some break down an important type of food you eat called fiber. You eat fiber when you eat delicious foods such as apples and oatmeal.

Good germs also help protect your body from bad germs, but if too many bad germs get inside your tummy, they can make your tummy ache.

102.02

Bad germs can make you very sick.

They can make you use the bathroom a lot.
Sometimes they make you vomit or throw up.

UUGH!!!
BLEHHH......

Most bad germs live outside your body. They live on things you touch.

29

They live on door knobs.

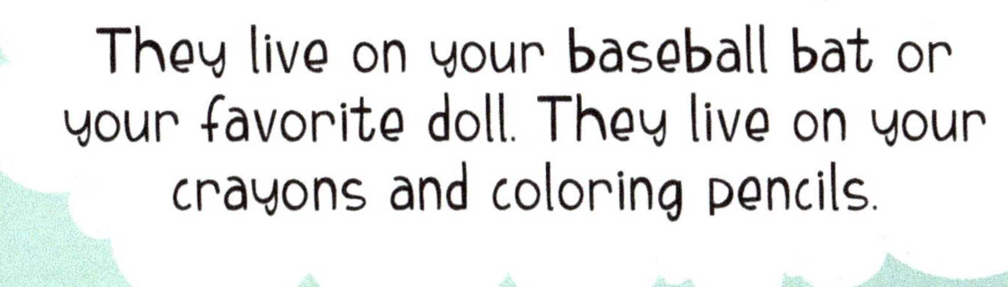

They live on your **baseball** bat or your favorite doll. They live on your crayons and coloring pencils.

Do you know how bad germs get inside your body? Touching and playing with anything that has bad germs on it puts the bad germs on your hands.

If too many bad germs get on your hands and
you put your hands in your mouth or eat food
with your hands, these bad germs can get inside
your tummy.

The best way to keep bad germs out of your tummy is to wash your hands with soap and warm water before you eat.

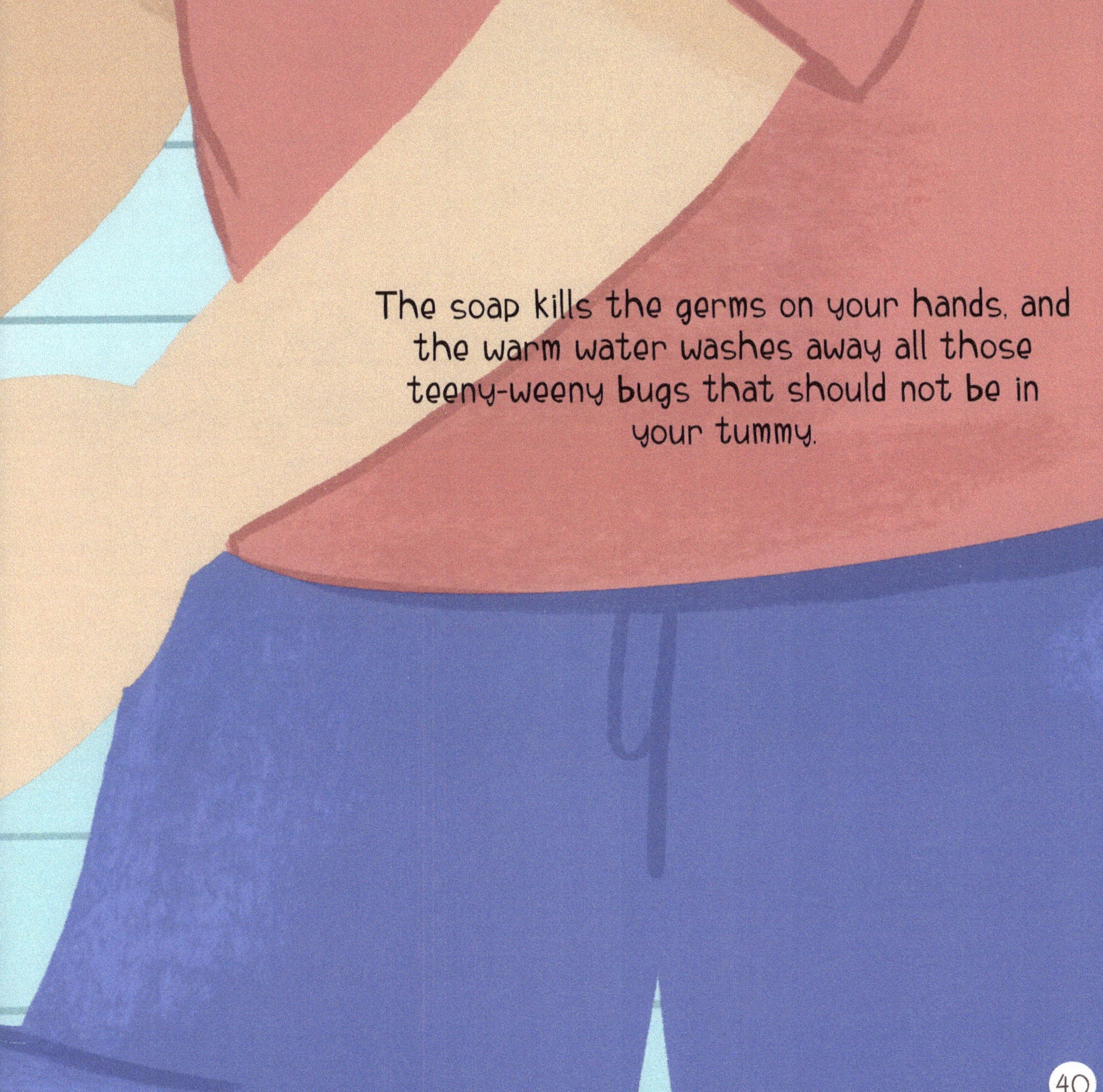

The soap kills the germs on your hands, and the warm water washes away all those teeny-weeny bugs that should not be in your tummy.

The next time you go to eat, remember there are bad bugs on your hands, and good bugs in your tummy. Wash your hands to wash away the bad germs so you won't get bad bugs in your tummy.

Follow these steps

1. Wet your hands with clean, running water—either warm or cold.

2. Apply soap and lather well.

3. Rub your hands vigorously for at least 20 seconds. Remember to scrub all surfaces, including the backs of your hands, wrists, between your fingers, and under your fingernails.

4. Sing your favorite nursery rhyme. Try Twinkle, Twinkle Little Star or one verse of Mary Had a Little Lamb. This will help you make sure you've scrubbed your hands long enough.

5. Rinse well, then dry your hands with a clean towel or air-dry them.

When should I wash my hands?

You should wash your hands:

- After you use the bathroom

- After you sneeze or cough

- Before you eat any food

- Anytime you know your hands are dirty